Plot 37

An Allotmenteer's firs

Plot 37 is an account of my journey, evolving from a novice gardener to a proficient 'Allotmenteer' in just one year.

I'd like to share with you the experience of discovering a hobby that will enhance your lifestyle, last a lifetime and give you a new found appreciation of nature and a sense of pride in creating something from nothing.

Along the way you can share my humour, successes and frustrations as I transform a desolate council allotment plot into a structured and fertile growing machine that is producing quality vegetables and flowers all year around. I will talk you through the principles of constructing an allotment and guide you through the pitfalls of creating an allotment.

During a night of boring television I began channel hopping to find something interesting to watch as I sprawled on the couch like the proverbial potato once again. By chance I stumbled upon a gardening programme called Gardeners world on the BBC and became interested in a piece being presented by the host Monty Don on vegetable growing. As I watched him plant his seeds another seed began to germinate in my head – I could get an allotment!

The rest as they say 'Is history!' – read on.......

Acknowledgements

- Cover Illustration supplied by Simon Howden Photographer

- Courtesy of www.Freedigitalohotos.net

- Thank you to my wife Catherine for putting up with me!

- Thanks to my lovely daughter Ellie for helping me on the plot.

- Thanks to my allotment buddies – Alan, John & Eleanor and Colin.

- Thanks to my Jack Russell Kipper for just being there!

In search of Eden

It was February and a year had passed since I had initially applied for an allotment with the local council. I knew that there was a site just a five minute walk from home hidden away on the outskirts of my village, although I had never been there I was aware that behind the high galvanised perimeter fencing there was an allotment site as I had often seen people coming and going when I had been going past it as I walked the dog. Little did I know that a unique self sufficient micro community existed within the vast stockade?

It had taken so long that when the letter came inviting me to attend a site viewing I almost didn't go – as they say 'The moment had gone'. Thankfully curiosity got the better of me and I arranged time off work to attend the site viewing. I rang the council to confirm my intention to attend and spoke to the council clerk a very pleasant woman called Rachael. After a little polite small talk I discovered that I was second on the waiting list and there were more than two plots available, so one way or another I would get a plot – brilliant!

The day came and I arrived at the gates at 09:00 as instructed and was surprised to see a group of about a dozen people patiently waiting and making polite conversation as they awaited Rachael from the council. I joined their ranks and gave a few tentative nods to those who had made eye contact. I began to feel quite smug as I listened to them fathom out the pecking order of the waiting list of those present. A guy called Steve was organising the lottery and when I told them I was second on the list my status seemed to rocket!

After striking up conversation with some of the group it became evident that most of us had been on the waiting list for ages and at this stage we had no idea how many plots were actually available. I discovered that in our district - plots became available once per year when the rents were due and people vacated or simply vanished into the ether.

Eventually Rachael arrived with her clip board and began to call out the names on the register to confirm who had arrived, I was having a flash back to my schooldays. After she had finished calling out the names she apologised and explained that we would have to wait for five minutes as somebody was delayed

3

and were on their way. After another ten minutes of waiting a young woman came hurtling down the lane on a bicycle with her long hair streaming in the wind as she pedalled like a bat out of hell towards us. She dismounted and breathlessly apologised for being late. Rachael produced the keys for the large padlock and the large galvanised gates swung open. As I watched her lead on - the situation reminded me of Willy Wonka welcoming everyone into the chocolate factory, fingers crossed I had a golden ticket – but life's never quite like that is it?

As we walked around the site I was shocked at what I saw as we passed the individual plots. My idyllic vision of well tended gardens complete with picket fences and potting sheds was shattered in an instant. The collection of ramshackle knock up sheds, tin roofs, pallet fences and junk reminded of a shanty town that had been abandoned and all of a sudden I was having doubts. I noticed a few people within the group exchanging glances and they were evidently feeling the same way.

As we walked along Rachael explained the selection criteria. We were to visit each available plot and take a few minutes inspecting each of them. Then after inspection - plots would be claimed in list order, however plots could be claimed as we went along but once the decision was made you couldn't change your mind. The very first plot we arrived at could not be seen from the pathway as it was completely fenced in. You could see from the outside that it had a large building made of brick near the gate which looked in a good state of repair – a hen house or secure shed maybe?

As she opened the gate I was shocked to find a little oasis with a flagstone pathway running down the middle, turned over, weed free and freshly tilled soil complete with plum trees and apple trees dotted around the plot – guess who was just about to miss out on this one! The apparition that had just arrived on the bike turned out to be first on the list and duly claimed her prize with immediate effect. At this point I seriously considered requesting a stewards enquiry as she had arrived late after all, if she'd only had a puncture or a minor none life threatening crash on her bike – I would have been in Eden by default; alas I returned to my senses and conceded into gentlemanly defeat, congratulating her by saying 'You've dropped on their love' which was my diplomatic reflex suppressing the urge kick her spokes in! Oh well maybe my Eden was further up the path just waiting for me – lead on Rachael, lead on!

We walked along and I eagerly surveyed the plots as we went wondering which would become mine. We walked past several that were untended with weeds growing freely but we weren't offered them, I would find out in the future that some of the plots were occupied but not worked – more of that later.

After passing every plot many overgrown along the pathway without offer we arrived at the corner. To the left Rachael pointed to what looked like a small section of woodland complete with Elderberry trees, brambles, nettles and piles of refuse and glass, you could also make out various mounds of masonry, bricks and general rubbish which was open at the front with no fencing, this was evidently being used as the dumping ground for the site. I was shocked when Rachael stated that this forgotten land was actually two plots. She looked at me expectantly as I asked if the council would be providing a JCB and the skips required to clear the site – her expression changed as she politely replied no. I asked how she expected us to have a chance of clearing that lot without machinery and waste disposal but I could tell that I was knocking on wood as her thousand yard stare pierced through me. I've never been afraid of hard graft but there was no way I was tackling that and as the group began to look at each other in disappointed realisation nor were they. As the mood changed within the group we walked in silence to the next available plots that were around the corner. This was another corner plot without fencing. It wasn't quite as bad as the one before but it was bad enough – needless to say I didn't jump in and claim my prize. At this point a weathered looking chap arrived complete with a woolly hat and wellies on; it transpired that he was the site secretary - a long serving tenant that had been elected at some point to oversee the site. He informed Rachael that plot 37 had become vacant further back down the path. Rachael consulted her clip board and told him that she had no record of it. The secretary assured her that the site had been vacated although it appeared that the council records hadn't been updated yet. Knowing that I had the first refusal of the plots remaining I asked if it would be possible to inspect it with a view to having the first refusal when it became vacant. Rachael begrudgingly agreed and we went to the plot. At this stage I had my fingers crossed as I knew that if this one wasn't suitable I was about to bin the whole idea and grow potatoes in a plastic bin in the back garden.

I couldn't believe my luck when the secretary 'Johnny' pointed to a plot that had a brand new five foot high fence along the front that was constructed out of double lapped boards and freshly treated with wood stain – at this point I didn't care what was on the inside I was having it! The plot to the left of it looked overgrown and vacant, as it didn't have a gate on we all entered via that entrance as there wasn't a fence between the plots. Although plot 37 was overgrown with weeds and grassland in comparison to the others it had potential and the debris scattered around the site could be composted or burnt which would save a fortune on skips – I heard myself state 'I'll take it' Rachael cautioned that the plot wasn't officially available yet but Johnny reassured her that it would be, however until official confirmation came through it wouldn't be released. I said that I would take the chance as the other plots weren't suitable for me. I looked at Johnny and he winked at me – I had found my Eden! It took another eight weeks for the confirmation to come through but after a lot of phone calls and pestering I got the keys to the kingdom!

Once I got my keys I went straight down and conducted a full 'recce' of my new garden. The plot to the right had a six foot boundary fence between us that looked good but the boundary to the left was open adjoining an overgrown and neglected plot that resembled a jungle. My plot wasn't much better covered in grass, weeds and the remnants of a chicken run surrounded by chicken wire and rotten posts. The overall plot was 24 ft wide by 128 ft long – 3072 sq ft of weeds and it was all mine what the hell I was going to do with it – I had no idea!

Tentatively I began to explore the plot. I could see the chicken run at the bottom, numerous wooden pallets, pieces of old wood and a wheelie bin and rubbish were everywhere. I recognised the dock leaves which I thought may come in handy as I waded through the swathes of stinging nettles that were licking at my ankles. In the centre of the plot I found a small tree that transpired to be a Gooseberry bush. It was surrounded by a circular ring of old bricks as if it was a monument so I knew it wasn't a giant weed – I would later find out exactly what it was once I had set fire to it as one of the old timers on the site explained to me that I had just destroyed the finest Gooseberry bush on the allotments – I just thought that the brick circle around it would make a good fire pit!

The plot was south facing which I knew was a bonus; however the land was on an incline from south to north which was quite steep maybe a drop of about 5ft from top to bottom, which had the potential to be a frost pocket at the bottom.

I began to wander when my neighbours either side would show up and then I suddenly had a sense of trepidation as it dawned on me that I didn't have a clue what I was doing. I had always cut the grass at home, dug the borders and made the annual pilgrimage to B & Q for the plants and plugged them in to the soil but that was the limit of my gardening prowess – this was a whole new ball game and I suddenly began to feel exposed!

I shook off the feeling by reasoning to myself that the people to the right of me obviously knew what they were doing as their plot was immaculate, complete with vegetables growing and free range chickens ambling around inside their pens so they would probably be nice to get along with. But the people to my left were just good at growing weeds and had either died and not bothered to tell the council or had won the lottery and buggered off. Either way their plot looked like mine so in my book that made us even – game on!

Over the coming days I decided that the logical thing to do was to tidy everything up and burn what I couldn't use. I didn't want chickens as working twelve hour shifts four on four off would make it impractical so I stripped down the chicken run. During this time I devoured every book on vegetable gardening that I could find on my Kindle and found a new mentor in Alan Titchmarsh who's books offer real practical advice – that's where I discovered Glysophate to kill the weeds or to the novice 'Round – Up'. The idea is that you spray all the weeds grass included and the chemical kills the weed down to the roots over a period of time without poisoning the soil. However it soon became evident that this took too long and the easiest and quickest way to clear a plot is to buy, hire or borrow a petrol strimmer complete with industrial strength line and take the vegetation right down to the soil. Over a week or so I had transformed my overgrown plot to a blank canvas of brown soil waiting to be dug over; I was impressed with my handy work although a little deaf from the strimmer. I kept burning off the vegetation and waste wood on my plot and often found myself sitting on the stack of pallets I had saved, watching the flames realising that it was like being a kid again on bonfire night – brilliant!

Ground Zero

The land I had cleared suddenly looked vast, far bigger than it had looked when it was covered by weeds and rubbish. I had a real sense of achievement and by now I had been introduced to some of my neighbours who had remarked that they were impressed with the way I was cracking on. During these conversations I was given a history of the allotments and informed that my allotment and the two adjoining ones were once the stomping ground of the 'legend' called Old Albert. Apparently this chap had tended the plots for years and had single handedly hand dug every square inch of ground until old age had caught up with him. According to folk lore he was a master grower and was renowned for producing show winning produce – a hard act to follow but at least the soil must be fertile I thought.

I explained outright that I was a complete novice which seemed to surprise them. Within days I had people bringing me young plants to get me started. Wave after wave of trays were brought over by my neighbours and then one day out of the blue I was invited over to John and Eleanor's plot for coffee with the others – I'd arrived and it felt great!

As I got to know my neighbours it became apparent that between them they had vast experience and would transpire to be far more valuable to me than Alan Titchmarsh (no offence Alan but you just weren't there!). As we approached spring time I began to admire the crops that they had growing, the work that had gone into them and a new found appreciation of recycling. Nothing goes to waste on an allotment a use can be found for most things that are readily discarded domestically.

If you want to clear a plot properly and prepare it to grow vegetables and flowers there is no way of avoiding having to dig out the weeds. The chemical method has merit but it takes far too long and if rain happens to fall within a few days of application it will basically become ineffective. I originally bought my petrol strimmer to simply take the top of the vegetation. I bought the recommended strimmer line but became really frustrated at how often it broke and forced me to stop and rewind the line. After speaking to one of the lads on the site who was an ex landscape gardener he told me that you could buy industrial strength line that was far more effective than the nylon line I was using although it was a little more expensive. I jetted off to B & Q in the car and found a 50 meter reel of the line for £18 which I thought was expensive but I took a chance, it worked out to be the best £18 spent so far. The line looks like electrical wire and it whizzes around like a bull-whip. Instantly I realised that as well as totally decimating the vegetation if I angle the strimmer a little - the line took the vegetation right down to the soil. Within thirty minutes I looked back at my handy work and realised I had just had a stroke of luck. Every so often I raked the vegetation to a pile ready to burn off later. I still have some of the strimmer line left over so it proved to be real value for money after all.

When it comes to digging be prepared for some hard physical graft. Although in my youth I had done labouring jobs including digging up the roads for the gas board – for the last twenty years the heaviest things I had lifted was the phone in my office. The secret to digging is to accept that you will ache all over the next day and you will get sore patches on your hands and sometimes blisters if you're not careful – but if you approach the task sensibly the latter effects can be lessened to a tolerable level. The main thing is to set realistic targets based on your own capabilities and take your time. Once you begin stop frequently to catch your breath - remember it's not a job, it's a hobby and you are your own master. Once you become attuned to the work you will find your own rhythm and after a little practice you may find that the exercise is quite enjoyable. After all you will be taking exercise in the best gym in the world and you don't have to wear spandex – unless you want to!

The tools you use for digging over are really important and the correct choice can make the job easier or harder if you get it wrong. The two main tools are a spade and fork either full sized or smaller sized referred to as border sized. The other key choices are handle, shaft and metal construction. The handles are available in two main types a T handle or a D handle. I prefer the D type handle as when using the T type my fingers are separated when levering down which I find uncomfortable and can also cause blisters between the fingers as well as on the palms of the hand, whereby my grip is improved with the D type as my fingers are together when pulling down. To avoid the hand blisters wear a glove on the hand that you grip the handle with. The blisters are caused by the friction of the handle against your skin, the glove acts as a barrier.

The length of the shaft is also important especially if you're tall – so choose wisely. After buying the wrong tools for myself initially I have settled on ash wood handled kit with stainless steel metalwork. The stainless steel cuts into the earth more effectively and the dirt also slides off easier if the soil is wet and 'claggy' I also find that there is better flex in the wooden handles compared to the plastic composite ones I have tried so far. Having said that there are now ergonomically designed composite handles on the market whereby the handle is angled to provide more leverage – which looks quite good, although I haven't tried one yet.

By working on a section at a time you can quickly turn the ground over removing the weeds as you work along. I found that by splitting the site into small sections it was easier to feel a sense of achievement and at times when I get tired or lack focus I will drift off and do a little pottering about until I feel 'rejuvenated' and return to the job. Over time I have found the technique of drifting off and doing other tasks to be pretty useful to stop myself getting fed up and bored. Sometimes especially on sunny days or late evenings it's very satisfying to just sit, relax and enjoy the view. It was during one such moment of relaxation that I realised that it was great to be outdoors again instead of being stuck in the house and enduring the routines of sleep, work, shopping and generally running around like a headless chicken going nowhere or alternatively wasting away in front of the television. It may sound melodramatic but I began to feel alive again and more importantly at peace with myself – who would have thought that! Without a shadow of doubt as the months went on I began to feel better in myself, I was also toning up and losing weight as well. I had inadvertently found a haven where I had my own space and could become so engrossed that life's problems faded away.

Once the ground has been dug over roughly and the weeds have been removed it's time to improve the soil – to the novice add manure. As it was the middle of spring and I was keen to get growing something - I opted to use chicken manure pellets. The pellets are high in nitrogen which is good for most vegetables especially brassicas. The most effective way to improve the soil structure is to add horse manure in the autumn and leave it for the worms and weather to break down. But to get up and running quickly pellets do an effective job, I also found out that my Jack Russell has a liking for them which I find disturbing!

Plot Design

When I first started out I hadn't given any thought to the impracticality of cultivating the soil completely by hand. I hadn't even considered the necessity of a rotavator to till the soil to a fine tilth suitable for planting. I soon realised that there is a marked difference between digging a few flower beds by hand in a small garden to working over 3000 sq ft of neglected soil that had the consistency of bell metal when dry.

I didn't have the budget to buy a rotavator initially or the means to transport one around in any case, so at this stage I had a dilemma. I could have borrowed one but as these machines are really expensive I preferred to be self sufficient. Whilst browsing e-bay I discovered mini rotavator's called 'Mantis' they are small, portable and light and can be easily transported around in the boot of the car with the handles folded down. I watched a video of the little machines in action on You Tube and was impressed with their ability to till the soil into a fine consistency. The machine fitted my needs and my pocket as I eventually managed to purchase one via e-bay for £90 which was a great buy considering that a new one retails at around £300.

To get the best from any cultivator you must break the soil up with a fork otherwise the tines of the machines will just bounce off the ground without effect. It is also a good idea to water the soil the night before to help soften the ground up. The machines then work their way through the soil grinding it into a powder ready for planting – magic!

Most of the plots on site had a path running along one side and were then fully dug in the middle, making maximum use of the land available. As I had worked along I began to toy with the idea of making raised beds as I just couldn't make sense of what I was going to plant and where. It is probably due to an early onset of 'OCD' but my brain seemed to work better with the idea of having small separate sections, rather than the standard fully dug plot. I reasoned that it would also be easier to work out a crop rotation plan – the only sticking point was that I didn't have enough timber to build the beds and I didn't want to spend a fortune on purchasing new wood, however the idea had set in my mind and as the saying goes necessity is the mother of all invention!

The idea of raised beds is to provide order and structure to a plot but more importantly to create a deep bed full of softly tilled topsoil that isn't walked upon. They are easier to plant up, manage and tend. My first attempt at raised beds was by using reclaimed pallet boards, which I obtained from a local pallet yard for 20 pence each for a 4ft length which I thought was good value, I purchased a few lengths of 2x2 inch and cut them down to make the stakes to screw the boards onto and constructed the first bed at 12ft x 4ft and it looked quite good but didn't feel quite right.

The next bed I tried was constructed in the same way but I used new decking boards which were easier to construct as they were in 8ft lengths and this time I constructed a larger bed at 16ft x 8ft. This cost me around £36, far more expensive than the first one but the timber is tanalised which should resist rot for at least ten years. By trial and error I have found that the best timber to use for raised beds is used scaffolding planks. They come in various lengths right up to 13ft and are 9 inches wide. They can be are more expensive to purchase but from a construction perspective they are easier to assemble and far more sturdy as at 13ft there is no need for any middle joints, they are also treated to withstand rotting.

I began to work along the plot digging, constructing and planting up the beds as I went. Before I knew it the plot was transforming and the feeling of achievement was heartening. My confidence was growing and so was my very first home grown vegetables, cabbages, cauliflowers, Swede and Potatoes had all begun to spring into life from the gifts of young plants that my new found friends had given me earlier.

By chance I discovered that the father of an old school friend had the allotment adjacent to mine. I hadn't seen my old school chum for over thirty years when one day he arrived in a flat back transit to visit his dad. After a warm reunion he came onto my plot to look at my efforts. It was then that he told me that he ran his own paving and fencing business and offered to furnish my paths with reclaimed paving flags, as to him they were a waste product that he had to pay to dispose of – talk about a stroke of luck! Over the coming months he gave me hundreds flag stones and even delivered me enough fencing panels to complete the boundary fence between me and the jungle next door – this transformed my plot and I will be forever grateful to him – thank you 'Riley' .

Another benefit of starting an allotment is realising the sense of community that exists within them. People of all ages, abilities and different social backgrounds become friends in a way that would not necessarily happen normally within ordinary life. I have found that if you are prepared to be pleasant towards people by saying a simple hello, you will be surprised by how soon you become accepted into their fraternity, especially if you get stuck into your plot and prove that you are serious about the venture and not just another passer by indulging in the latest craze for a few weeks.

During the first few weeks I got know another neighbour called Alan. Alan had two adjoining plots with a large chicken run at the bottom. His plot was crammed with all varieties of vegetables, fruit trees and raspberry canes, complete with four greenhouses full of tomatoes, chillies cucumbers and melons. By looking around his plot I picked up ideas to use in my own. Alan had been on the site for over seven years and it was obvious that he was an expert grower. He also came to be a valued friend and I soon realised that he was predisposed to help anyone. He seems to have friends and contacts for everything. Over the early months he has gone out of his way to collect horse manure and my first greenhouse on his trailer for me, all provided through his friends and acquaintances free of charge – a true friend. His selfless practical help and advice along with that of my old school friend mentioned previously have undoubtedly put me well in advance of where I would have been on my own.

As I got to know Alan he explained that many of the plots his included had the dreaded Club root on them. This is a plant disease that affects the Brassica family and basically deforms the roots preventing them from growing properly resulting in either failed or poor crops. Once the spores of the disease enter the soil it is difficult to get rid of and can remain within the soil for over twenty years. So far I have discovered that I have it in a small corner of one of my beds where I was growing summer cabbages.

After a short while I realised that I had turned into a bit of a Magpie. I had begun to collect all sorts of things that I thought we be of use on the plot. Timber, scaffold planks, plastic barrels – your mind seems to subconsciously switch into re-cycling mode. Once the word was out, friends, family and neighbours were offering me all sorts of items that I gratefully accepted.

Planting Time

Although I had been given a lot of plants from my new friends I wanted to grow some of my own. The traditional way to grow on the allotment is to sow the seeds directly into well prepared soil which can be easier and less time consuming than sowing into seed trays, however there are draw backs to both methods as I discovered. When I sowed directly the weeds inevitably came and at times I couldn't tell the difference between the plants and the weeds. When I sowed into trays I had the problem of 'pricking out'. As the seedlings develop their roots become entangled with each other and the term pricking out means to separate them and transplant into larger pots to grow on. It may sound easy enough to do in principal but I find it a fiddly chore. I prefer to sow into seed modules which are plastic seed tray with individual cells to hold a single seed to create a plug plant. The trays are inexpensive and some can hold up to 150 plugs per tray. The plants can be grown to a size that is easy to handle (and recognise). Once the plants have reached four to five inches in height they are ready to be planted out into the main bed.

One tip I that I have picked up is to cover the young plants with mini cloche's made from 2 litre pop bottles. This keeps the pigeons off and the slugs out until the plants have time to establish themselves within the bed. The wind is kept at bay and a micro climate is created that is beneficial to the plant. I leave the tops off to let air in and make it easier to water however some people elect to put the tops on to form an impenetrable barrier for the slugs – although unscrewing them each time that you want to water would be too much of a hassle for me.

I have had good results using this method and costs nothing; just put the word out that you are collecting them and you will still have a collection to use. Simply cut off the base of the bottle and place over the plant and gently twist the bottle into the soil until it feels sturdy enough to withstand the wind. Leave them in place until the plants begin to outgrow them and then remove and clean for storage. You will also be doing your bit for re-cycling – easy!

Friend or Foe

There is no finer feeling than to sit back and admire your allotment once the construction is finished and your juvenile plants begin to grow. As row after row of organic produce begins to flourish a primal sense of satisfaction of being able to produce food for the family really kicks in. The trouble is that you have also created an excellent alfresco restaurant for every bug, slug and bird within the district and believe me they will come to dinner!

When I set out on this venture I was determined to grow organically (and I still am in principal) as I didn't want to poison the produce that my family were going to eat with who knows what kind of chemicals or indiscriminately kill beneficial insects as well as pests. However after watching hundreds of caterpillars decimate my prized cabbages in a matter of weeks my resolve to remain organic was severely tested. At one stage I would have gladly called in an airstrike of Napalm just to spite the buggers if I could have!

Over that first summer I witnessed at first hand the destructive power of insects and pigeons as wave after wave of them began to attack my hard earned produce and left me with a feeling of 'what's the point?'

Firstly the Wood Pigeons shredded the tender plants as soon as I removed the pop bottles that had held them at bay for so long. They must have been watching for weeks on end as their meals developed just waiting for the moment to strike and strike they did. I remember removing the bottles from a row of summer cabbages one Friday night before I went home. When I returned the next morning all that remained was the skeleton of stems and leaves. They looked like a row of miniature trees that had endured a nuclear blast!

Later in the year the next major problem occurred when cabbage white butterflies came into season and began to prowl. Before the attack I recall seeing the garden fill will beautiful butterflies fluttering around the garden. I remember feeling a tranquil sense of ease as they flew around and began to feel at one with nature – I was being fooled believe me!

A few weeks 'they' arrived. Battalions of yellow and black striped alien creatures began to crawl everywhere as the caterpillars began to reach maturity – there was no stopping them. They began to chew through anything leaving their faeces deposited within the leaves as they went and I swear the leaves of the plants became thread bare before my eyes – I couldn't believe it!

There were so many of them that the situation began to get out of control and we were all in danger of losing the majority of our produce. Butterflies lay their eggs on the underside of the plant leaves most of the time which makes them difficult to locate. The eggs are bright yellow and are laid in clusters about the size of a fingertip. The first line of defence against them is to regularly inspect the plants for the eggs or small larvae and destroy them by squashing them between your fingers. But try as you might you won't find them all I assure you.

It was during this time of plague and pestilence that I realised that if farmers didn't use pesticides it would be impossible to feed the majority of the planet on an industrial scale. But for the domestic grower it is possible if you are prepared to take some practical steps and concede that you will lose a few battles along the way to winning the war.

First of all barrier methods can be used to prevent the insects landing on the vegetables in the first place. Most widely used is netting. I now use scaffolding netting which has a fine mesh and makes it difficult for the butterflies to penetrate it – but not impossible. I drape the netting over canes and seal the edges with soil to weight it down from the wind and prevent entry by the pests.

In addition to netting it is still important to go hunting for the insects and kill on site. Either squash them or feed them to the hens but I wouldn't recommend throwing them over the fence – they will come back!

Another method is to spray with a homemade organic pesticide. These can be made from various concoctions ranging from onions to chillies and most can be effective if made strong enough. Another ingredient often referred to in gardening books is soft soap or to you and me washing up liquid. Although not strictly organic this stuff definitely works, killing the caterpillars within a few minutes of contact. Apparently the liquid blocks their ability to breathe by sticking to the skin and then they curl up and die – job done! I would also recommend that you get a spray dispenser with a wand type applicator. They are easier to use as you don't have to keep pumping the trigger and the long handle means that you don't have to get down on your knees as much.

For a non organic option I can recommend 'Resolver Bug Spray' this definitely works quickly and effectively and is useful if things get out of hand.

For slug control I have always used slug pellets but I am now switching to beer traps made from pots and jars sunken into the soil and filled with beer or lager. The slugs are attracted to the beer, crawl in and drown – everybody's happy!

The battle against bugs is constant, if you falter with your regime of protection they will undoubtedly win. Aim to recruit help in the fight by attracting a selection of nature's mercenaries. Birds, hedgehogs and a myriad of insects can be tempted in to the plot if you provide the right conditions for them to feed and nest. This small army of Special Forces can be really effective in the battle to save your crops and remain as organic as possible.

As you work the soil you will begin to notice beetles spiders and centipedes scuttling around the plants and burrowing into the soil. Whatever you do try not to kill them as these little fellows are some of your best assets. This is one of the major problems of using insecticides that don't differentiate between the good guys and bad ones. Once the balance of beneficial insects is disrupted nature has difficulty replenishing them back to effective levels and then there are no marines on the beach when the next batches of invaders descend!

It is useful to be able to identify the different species within the garden as some are pests like wireworm that burrow into your prized potatoes mercilessly drilling holes into the tubas as they grow.

Another weapon in the arsenal against unwanted pests is companion planting. This method of prevention could fill a book itself and many very good sources of information are available but in short it is the art of growing plants that either attract predators to kill pest insects, form barriers in terms of scent that pests detest or the last line of defence to draw the enemy away by attracting them to plant species that are not vegetables this method is referred to as 'catch cropping' the insects can be tempted away to an area where they will congregate in large numbers where they can be ambushed and despatched. A plant I have success with are Nasturtiums these leafy plants produce cascades of red, yellow and orange flowers that look lovely along a fence line and they attract black flies away from the crops.

French Marigolds are also invaluable as a companion plant they work particularly well to protect potatoes and tomatoes. Their roots exude a chemical scent that deters slugs and there flower scent definitely deters flies. Last season I planted four plant in the greenhouse borders and I don't recall seeing one fly or insect in there apart from the odd stray Bee – even when the door had been left open all day.

Weeds are another form of pest. Once the conditions are right these monsters are difficult to eradicate, relentless and designed by nature to survive almost anything. If N.A.S.A. sent a tray of weeds to Mars I swear that the planet would be green within a month!

My new mates on the allotment introduced me to a brilliant tool to combat them it's called a 'Speed Hoe' the head of the hoe is shaped like a shield that has blades sharpened around all edges. By head is angled to be parallel to the ground and by moving it backwards and forwards across the soil it easily decapitates the weeds just below the soil surface – it takes minutes to cover large sections of ground. On a hot day the head of the weed can be left to shrivel in the sunshine – job done!

When it comes to weeds prevention is better than the cure. Where practical to do so the best option is to plant through weed suppressant sheeting. It keeps the light out which prevents them from germinating but is designed to let water through into the soil. There are various types of liner ranging in quality and price to suit all budgets and even the cheapest versions will easily last a year and save you your valuable time.

Another method that I'm trialling at the moment is organic mulching. One of the plot holders is a Tree Surgeon and the shredded by product from his work forms an organic barrier that can be spread deeply over the beds to keep out the light. By utilising a combination of the latter methods, weeding time is reduced.

Composting & Fires

Without doubt you will need to create an area for composting and somewhere safe to build a bonfire. Composting is an important part of organic gardening and will become the engine room for the allotment over time.

Compost bins can be purchased or made it is down to personal preference. There are plastic ones that resemble Daleks from Dr Who or wooden ones that can be purchased. Better still wooden enclosures can be made from reclaimed timber or wooden pallets. The best system consists of three bays that allow for old and new material to be amassed and turned over periodically into the empty bay.

There is a system for effective composting that requires a mixture of green and brown material to be layered alternately. Basically the green material is things like cabbage leaves and potato peel etc and the brown material is plain cardboard egg boxes and woody material. Too much of one or the other material will stall the composting process. Once the balance is right heat begins to generate as the microbes begin to devour the waste product. Activators can be added to assist the process such as chicken manure or you can buy activating mix that has the same effect.

You will also find that hundreds of small red earthworms begin to arrive within the heap and assist with the decomposition process. They are also pretty useful for any anglers out there. The resulting mixture of dark compost is a fantastic soil improver and is commonly referred to as black gold. No allotment is complete without a compost heap. The sheer amount of inedible waste product from the produce at harvest time is surprising. By utilising effective composting nothing goes to waste it is simply recycled and put back into the earth to begin the whole process again. During a growing season enough material can be collected to provide quality compost for the following year. Domestic waste can be utilised as well as material from the plot, however never put cooked food or raw meat into the heap unless you want to attract vermin.

There are parts of the plants that are impractical to compost such as Brassica stalks etc that would take too long to break down naturally. This is where the fire pit comes in handy. By burning the material down the ash can be spread directly onto the soil and dug in and used as a soil improver, however avoid burning plastics if you intend to spread the ash onto the soil as you will be contaminating it.

Most plot holders utilise forty five gallon drums to build fires in, some just burn directly upon the soil. I decided to build a fire pit out of brick which works better for me but ultimately the choice is yours.

When it comes to bonfires there are some simple health and safety rules, site rules and basic etiquette to avoid burning yourself and the site down and annoying fellow plot holders and or any adjacent homes that may be present near some sites. Firstly install a flag – you need to have an indication of the wind direction before you even begin to contemplate lighting a fire. The smoke that can be generated from a few cabbage leaves and kindling wood can be surprisingly acrid at times. The last thing that you want to do is smoke out your neighbours who have arrived on the site for a peaceful day at the plot. Some will suffer in silence but most will be quite vocal if you begin to suffocate them. If your site is adjacent to domestic properties it is wise to be especially aware of lighting fires. One letter of complaint to the local council or allotment landlord can cause you some major headaches which can be easily avoided by some simple courtesy.

When it comes to health and safety use common sense. Keep the fire small and under control. Always have a source of water handy either a hose or bucket just in case. Never repeat never pour petrol onto a fire either lit or unlit, although this sounds obvious it's easy to be tempted to give the fire a helping hand to get going but the results can be devastating.

If you adhere to the above you will be fine and there is nothing quite like sitting or standing by a fire and watching the flames – each time I light one it's like being a kid again. There is something primeval about making a fire and it never ceases to have a calming effect on me.

Some councils ban fires, others have strict rules that should be adhered to.

Health & Safety and Common Sense

Although the 'High Vis Vest Brigade' have gone wild over recent years banning everything from Kids playing conkers to insisting that everyone should wear a hard hat just in case a plane should fall out of the sky – some practical ways to avoid injury really do have merit, especially on the allotment.

Firstly always carry a mobile phone with you when visiting your plot. At times you may be the only person there and if you seriously injure yourself or become ill your allotment could prove to be a lonely place. Also ensure that you know the postal address of the site. I once had to help a fellow plot holder who was suffering from an epileptic fit and I had to direct the ambulance services by phone as travelled towards us, fortunately I knew the site address.

Most sites are fenced off and secured by locked gates. Make sure that you have a spare key cut for the entrance and it is left at home, that way your family will be able to get aid to you if you get into difficulties.

Purchase a basic first aid kit and keep it somewhere safe on the plot. By the nature of the jobs you will be doing cuts and blisters are inevitable. A bottle of anti septic hand gel is also useful.

A good selection of gloves for different jobs is useful to have. Thick Rigger type gloves are good for jobs such as paving or carrying brambles whilst more dextrous types are available for doing fiddly jobs around the plot. A good pair of quality safety shoes or boots is essential. If you don't have something with a sturdy sole you will run into difficulties as soon as you begin to dig as you begin to push the spade or fork into the soil. There is also the added hazard of old nails and shards of glass that could pierce an Elephants skin. Toe caps on your boots come in really handy when you drop your first flagstone on them – and you will!

When you begin to clear the plot you will encounter many hazards with various potential consequences. Brambles are great for springing back and catching you in the face. Goggles are a common sense must have accessory when working in thick undergrowth and mandatory when doing tasks such as strimming. Stones and glass fly like bullets and can do serious damage so don't take any chances.

Many plots have remnants of old buildings on them and in times gone by asbestos was the favoured material for building roofs. If you find any of this stuff my advice would be to avoid it like the plague. Call the council who will despatch a team of staff dressed in space suits and dispose of it as though it was nuclear waste – I kid you not, I don't know what is in this stuff but the authorities take its disposal very seriously and so should you.

There is nothing finer than spending a summer day working on the allotment. However there is danger lurking in the form of the Sun. Sunburn is not funny and can set you back for days if you're not careful. Even on overcast days you can become burned faster than you think when you spend extended periods outdoors. A good wide brimmed hat is advisable during the middle of the day and a good sun block is essential, especially on the back of the neck and arms.

It's also important to have clean drinking water available especially when you're doing heavy work as you can soon become dehydrated. It is sensible to ensure that you also have food available during long visits to keep up your energy levels. It's also nice just to sit and take a break whilst enjoying a cup of tea or coffee and a sandwich – you can admire your work whilst you recharge your batteries.

Ensure that you have somewhere comfortable to sit a folding deck chair will suffice and will feel like heaven when your especially hard at it. You may find yourself dropping off to sleep from time to time – go on enjoy it, it's not a job!

Watch out for the weather whilst you're on the plot. A summer day can soon turn into a summer storm complete with lightening quite quickly sometimes and you don't want to be caught outside with a metal rake in your hand when the lightning bolts start to fly. I was once on the plot during a lovely mild day when within ten minutes I was caught in the fiercest hailstorm that I have ever seen. When I first began to clear the plot I had no shelter at all. As I said previously I used to take my old fishing umbrella down with me to get out of the rain. One of your first priorities should be to construct or buy adequate shelter from the rain and sun preferably a shed. If I was starting again I would have simply bought a shed instead of deciding to build one myself out of packing crates and losing three weeks of my life that I'll never get back!

One of the least obvious hazards on the plot is garden canes; tripping over and impaling yourself is very distressing as I found out to my cost one day. If you use low level canes place a small pop bottle over the top or purchase the custom made caps that simply fit onto the top. It's easy to lose an eye if you fall over or end up with a body piercing that you hadn't counted on.

The most useful tool concerning hazards on the plot is common sense alas at times we even the best of us all forget or take unnecessary risks that can spoil your enjoyment. Don't take on any physical task that is beyond you capabilities. Sometimes you will need another pair of hands so arrange some help.

Chemicals such as weed killers and slug pellets should be stored away safely especially if children will be visiting the plot. Never leave cans of petrol on the plot as you may give the local kids something to light your shed up with if they come visiting and get bored one night.

And finally if you haven't had a Tetanus shot within the last ten years visit your Doctor and get one. If you have an existing medical condition such as epilepsy or diabetes let your fellow plot holders know as soon as you get to know them it could save your life. Fortunately and old chap on the site had told me that he had epilepsy and one day I noticed a whimpering noise that turned out to be him as he had collapsed onto some sheet glass suffering from convulsions. I managed to help him during a distressing time and get help to him quickly. I know that he would do the same for me if the situation was reversed and it's always good to know that others are watching your back.

Tools Buyer Beware

It is very easy to get carried away when buying tools for the allotment – I should know I've amassed everything known to man with the exception of a tractor but Christmas is coming soon!

Okay so I overdid it. In reality I have found that I need a Spade, Fork, Rake, Wheelbarrow, Secateurs, Knife, String, Bow saw, Hammer, Power drill, Hoe and a Trowel. The rest is junk.

Your tool selection is down to personal preference and I just love buying new stuff for the plot although I am slowing down a little now – you will find your own way.

When constructing things like fencing and sheds it is useful to have battery powered saws and drills to make the tasks easier but for run of the mill gardening the requirement for tools is essentially basic. Autumn and spring time will see you using the spade and fork. During the growing season you will never have the how out of your hands at times as you fight the weeds. The Wheelbarrow is a constant companion and can save you miles travelling up and down the plot. And the Trowel will be permanently by your side during planting.

Buckets are useful for collecting stones and glass that will be everywhere once you start to work the plot and prepare the beds.

You don't have to spend a fortune to be able to effectively work an allotment. You may be surprised how you are offered tools from friends and family once that they know you have a plot – mostly tackle that they have purchased on a whim that is cluttering up there shed at home and surplus to their requirements.

I was offered a long handled sledgehammer by a friend which I gratefully accepted; it came in very handy for knocking in the posts I needed to construct my fence.

Greenhouses the Engine Room

Although a Greenhouse isn't essential one does provide you with different growing options and adds another element to the experience of gardening.

I was fortunate enough to be offered one for free via a friend I have made on the allotment and its arrival has given me another sanctuary to potter around in. So far I have cultivated Tomatoes, Cucumbers, Peppers and Melons.

Greenhouses can be sourced second hand or new whichever suits your budget will do the trick. They can be glazed with glass or polycarbonate sheeting and either is effective, however I find that glass stands up to the elements a little better as the structure is more sturdy and stable. I initially glazed my roof with polycarbonate as when we collected it some of the glass panes had smashed during a storm. Once erected on the site we had a storm and the plastic panels just blew out due to them flexing in the wind, so I replaced them with glass and put the plastic along the front sides instead. Polycarbonate is safer to work with than glass and less likely to break if the local vandals decide to throw stones.

It's advisable to build the green house on a raised platform especially if you're tall. There's nothing worse than banging your head on the frame each time you enter or exit and raising the structure allows more height for those tomato plants. I mounted mine onto old railway sleepers; however the drawback is that you then have a step to contend with which can be a hazard in itself.

I elected to pave the centre of the floor and have three raised borders around the perimeter to grow my produce directly into the soil. Some people use grow bags but I read that soil is the best option and is better at water retention than pots or grow bags. I also planted Marigolds along the borders to deter flies and slugs. Another tip I picked up was to sink small pots into the ground near the roots of the tomato plants to enable water to reach the root systems directly.

Another benefit I have is that the previous owner had constructed a three tier custom made bench that was perfect for standing trays and pots upon. It is easy to remove during the growing season but I am now planning to leave it inside permanently as I now realise that I don't need the space for twelve tomato plants.

25

The greenhouse provides you with additional options for plant choices that may not necessarily thrive in our climate. It is also useful for getting seeds started early and cultivating things like hanging basket displays ready for the spring and summer. I constructed a goalpost structure to enable me to hang four baskets whilst they grew – it worked quite well. Once the baskets had been removed it served as a structure to secure gardens canes for my tomatoes and cucumbers to grow up.

I would caution that it is very easy to overproduce within the greenhouse. The first season I had tomatoes and cucumbers growing faster than I could eat them or give them away. Over a few months I furnished my friends family and strangers with produce and towards the end of the season I even fed next doors hens.

This year I intend to be more selective by trying different varieties in smaller volume which seems to be a more sensible approach to production. So far I have bought Roma, Brandy Boy, Alicante and Aisla Craig varieties to try which will provide a good selection of salad, beef and plum tomatoes which will cater for my families tastes and culinary needs for the season.

A useful edition to any greenhouse is an irrigation system. Due to work commitments I can't always visit the plot daily and in high summer this would be a problem to the survival of the tomato plants. The system comprises of a water bag or bladder that bolts onto the greenhouse frame. A system of flexible piping and leads to adjustable heads that drip feed water onto the base of the plants. The flow can be adjusted and the bladder holds enough water to last at least two days. The system was relatively inexpensive to buy and has proven to be good value for money.

It is important to make sure that your greenhouse has adequate ventilation to create airflow around your produce. Greenhouses usually have one or two vent openers in the roof and some also have Louvre windows placed along the sides. Automatic window openers can be installed which open when the temperature reaches a set level which can be adjusted manually. The openers are like small hydraulic arms that pivot and slowly push the vent window open and closed as required. These are especially useful on the allotment as many of us can't be there all the time, which would prove to be a disaster in some cases. I often left the greenhouse door open all the time especially around August time and whether by look or judgement didn't have any problems to speak of.

During the hottest times of the year it can also be beneficial to install shading within the greenhouse to protect the plants. This can be done by painting the inside of the glass with a purpose made wash or installing a system of mesh netting to lessen the effects of the Sun's rays entering the greenhouse. I use the fine mesh scaffolding netting which is easy to install and in my opinion looks better than smearing the glass with a substance that looks like white wash but as with everything it is down to personal preference.

Another piece of kit that is useful is the thermometer. After trialling a few inexpensive ones with relative success I eventually settled on the digital type. The unit displays the current temperature and also the highest and lowest recorded which remains on the display until you re-set it. The main benefit for me is to watch the lowest temperature to ensure that I have adequate insulation within the greenhouse during the colder months. If it gets too hot well the plants will be dead which would be self explanatory!

Regular feeding of greenhouse plants is essential once the fruit has begun to develop. Tomato feed is a substance high in Potash which is an essential nutrient for growth development and is readily available in liquid form. A few caps full are added to the watering can and is sufficient to sustain consistent growth. Homemade fertilisers can be made and are just as effective but for ease of use I elected to buy mine as it is inexpensive and lasts quite a long time and proves to be value for money. This type of feed has other uses outside of the greenhouse on strawberries and Raspberries for example. As with all food production regular feeding regimes will makes a real difference to the quality of the produce and coupled with regular watering patterns will provide you with top quality specimens fit for the table.

The possibilities to diversify your growing options afforded by having a greenhouse are invaluable. The structure also provides you with a place to work and potter around in if the weather is poor and you are unable to work outside. Once up and running you will discover that the greenhouse has become the engine room of your allotment.

Rules & Regulations

Different Councils and Landlords have varying regulations and rules that govern your tenancy as a plot holder. When you acquire your plot you will be required to sign a tenancy agreement which will state the duration cost and rules concerning your tenancy of the site. Please ensure that you fully read and understand the terms and conditions within the document as they are legally binding.

The site where I have my plot are very strict on the erection of buildings for example. Any plans for sheds or buildings have to be submitted to a planning committee for approval and must meet the detailed criteria written within the tenancy agreement. It can take a few weeks to gain approval for buildings as the committees will invariably only meet once per month. I received confirmation in writing for authorisation to build and position a shed on the plot. It is not worth taking the chance to build without permission as you may find that even though a building meets the criteria you may be forced to dismantle it due to disregarding the required authority. It's not worth the hassle so do things properly.

The keeping of livestock is another area that is regulated strictly. On our site we are allowed to keep Hens but no Cockerels, Rabbits and Geese anything else is not allowed. Apparently you were allowed to keep Pigs in years gone by but due to husbandry and slaughtering legislation the facility was removed by the council. If a plot is classified as a paddock horses may be kept. Each governing council or private Landlord will have their own restrictions on livestock and you should be aware of their requirements.

One major issue with keeping livestock is the presence of vermin that are attracted to the feed used in rearing them. Most Council sites provide Rodent control at regular intervals throughout the season to control the problem. At our site we are provided with bait boxes free of charge that are sealed and re-filled by licensed pest control experts at regular intervals. Whether you have livestock or not you will undoubtedly have vermin on the plot – even if you never see them yourself. I don't have livestock at the moment but my bait boxes are always empty each time the 'Rat Man' comes, although he has told me that it is mice that are frequenting my particular box.

Restricting the availability of loose feed, regular trapping and poison control are necessary requirements to control the problem. The last thing that residential areas need are rats running around all over the place. Local residents would soon be up in arms if rats were constantly running across their lawns or trying to join them for a barbeque in the summer and to be quite frank so would I in their position. I don't like rats and in reality that is another reason why I haven't bothered with raising chickens. I once saw one on a water treatment farm that was as big as my Jack Russell and I'd rather not see another one thank you very much!

The latter problems can be largely avoided if you follow a few simple rules. Don't leave feed out where vermin can access it and ensure that any stock is secured within sturdy containers such as plastic barrels with screw tops. Don't leave full troughs of chicken feed on the floor overnight. Only put enough food down to sustain the livestock that you hold. Regularly clean and inspect underneath and inside chicken huts and pens. Observing these simple steps can make a real difference and reduce the problems associated with rearing live stock. I have friends that observe good husbandry at the allotment site and their livestock are thriving.

Ensure that you protect yourself when you have vermin present especially rats. Wear gloves when working in those areas as rats carry Wiel's disease which is a bacteria carried within their urine. It can be contracted via cuts or direct contact with the eyes nose or mouth and in severe cases it can be fatal.

Plant Care

It may sound obvious but the regular watering and feeding of plants is essential and very easy to get completely wrong. Too much and they will die, too little and the result will be the same. It's easy to remember to water during hot or dry spells but more difficult to gauge when we've had a drop of rain.

The best indicator is to look at the soil just underneath the surface. If it appears to be dry water and give a decent soaking to the roots without drowning the plant. I have found that it is better to water thoroughly every two or three days than lightly sprinkling the surface daily. Too much water is as bad as too little but over time you will be able to gauge the requirements presented by the conditions.

I'm fortunate that one of the communal taps is directly outside of my plot. But even this isn't a reliable source at times as during the summer months it is in high demand and access to it is on a first come first served basis so a backup plan is required. There's nothing worse than coming home from work and planning a flying visit to water up before tea only to find that the other plot holders are siphoning it off by the gallon and making you wait. To combat this problem I acquired a 1000 litre tank from my friend Alan. I have it raised up high so that it is gravity fed and due to my plot being on a slope it has adequate pressure when I'm down at the bottom. Also have a water barrel near my shed to catch the rainwater and another down beside my greenhouse.

During my second season I had a poor potato crop that also developed scab. Small brown patches on the skin, which I later discovered was due to inadequate watering. Although at the time I thought that I had watered correctly I realised that the odd rain showers we had been getting were obviously not enough for this particularly thirsty crop. The potatoes were small in comparison to my first year's crop which seemed odd as my soil preparation during the second year was much better than the first. After discussing the matter with my friends on the site they told me that I had under watered. And then I realised I had been guilty of the same mistake across all of my crops. The cabbages were inferior to the first year and so on. As a result I know keep a record of when I water. I spend most of the day whizzing around with a million things on the go at once and it's easy to forget things. The logbook is a good aide memoir to me and I recommend it if you are similarly predisposed. It is also useful to log which varieties of vegetables do well on your particular plot. All gardens have their own micro climates and due to this some species will flourish where others don't. This is due to a combination of factors including soil type and condition light levels and wind conditions. A log will help you to discover which suits you best as you begin the process of trial and error season by season.

Good soil preparation can mean the difference between good crops and mediocre ones. Getting the soil PH correctly balanced is especially important to Brassica crops such as Cabbages, Cauliflowers and Swedes etc and it is simple to get right with a little time and patience. There are various soil testing kits that you can use or simpler devices that give an instant reading by pushing copper rods into the soil. I favour this method for its ease of use and instant results. For a few pounds the unit is adequate for my needs and if you remember to actually use it you will find that it is beneficial.

The next requirement for the plants is a regular feeding regime. People tend to realise that tomatoes need feeding, however the requirement to feed other crops is not necessarily a foregone conclusion to some – myself included initially. In short all crops benefit and thrive by providing them with appropriate supplemental feeding. Just like we benefit from taking vitamins, plants are just the same. The difference in plant health and growth rate is substantial by comparison. An all round fertiliser that seems to be favoured at our site is 'Growmore' this comes in a small pellet form and can be purchased in small or bulk quantities to suit your needs. The results of sprinkling just a few granules per plant each week are surprising and well worth the time and effort. Healthy plants are far better equipped to fight off disease and recover from pest attacks when they are in peak condition. The quality of the produce is also enhanced. There are also non commercial fertilisers that you can brew yourself such as Comfrey leaves and nettles. These plants contain high levels of nitrogen that are useful to Brassica's for example. Gather bunches of the plants and submerge them into a bucket of water and leave to brew for approximately six weeks. Ensure that the bucket has a lid because the resulting concoction really smells. Dilute a few capfuls into your watering can and feed weekly. The advantage is that it is free, organic and effective if you have the time to make it.

Growing Fruit

There are many varieties of fruit that can be successfully cultivated domestically if you have the right conditions. Fruit doesn't have to be rotated around the plot annually in the same way that vegetables do. Firstly you will need to select an appropriate site for things like Strawberry beds and Raspberry canes, preferably within a fruit cage to keep the birds from eating your prized fruits; however they can be netted off if installing a cage isn't a practical option.

A large strawberry bed can be propagated with a small initial outlay and minimal stock plants as each season the plant sends out runners which can be pinned into the soil from which another plant will grow for free. A strawberry plant will produce fruit within the first season and remain consistent over a period of three years before the natural production begins to subside and the plants will need to be replaced. Although I am told that they can produce far longer than that in certain conditions. The bed can be a permanent fixture and netting will be required. Always ensure that the netting is fine as small birds can become trapped. You also need to stretch the netting so that the net doesn't touch the fruit. Otherwise the birds will just perch on the net and feast on the fruit. I usually throw a few strawberries out to them periodically as at times it's like watching kids looking into a sweet shop window but there's enough to go around.

Raspberries will need a framework building to stretch wire across to tie in the canes as they grow. I built a simple goal post structure and got hook and eyes to enable me to tension the small gauge wire across to fasten to. Raspberries come in many varieties but they are basically classified into summer or autumn fruiting varieties. Summer fruiting types produce fruit on the previous season's canes whilst autumn fruiting varieties produce on the current year's growth. I elected to grow the autumn variety as I find the canes easier to manage. At the end of the season you simply cut all the canes to ground level and the whole process is easier to manage in my opinion. The fruit also arrives just in time to provide a tasty crop for jam making that is great on toast during those cold winter mornings.

This season I am going to add blackberries to the plot the thorn less variety which will fit neatly against a fence along the plot. I also have Victoria plum tree and Braeburn apple tree which are on dwarf rootstock.

Summary

Starting an allotment is a big undertaking and it is easy to underestimate the amount of effort and time that you will have to put into it during the initial years. I have seen many people come and go over the last two years that I have been on the allotment and to this day the plot next door to me has had three tenants that have all turned up with the best of intentions only to disappear after just a few weeks of hard graft got the better of them.

As I have explained with the right attitude, tools and a sensible approach you can soon turn a derelict plot into a fertile growing site. The cardinal rule is to remember that it isn't a job and when you find yourself getting tired or dismayed take a break from it for a few days and recover. There were many times during my initial build that I sat and thought to myself 'what the hell have I started' but I persevered and conquered it in the end and you can do the same!

I have created a space of my own to grow quality food for the family and discovered a pass time that I believe will last my lifetime. I've also made new friends and acquaintances that I would never had known otherwise.

Most notably for me I have discovered that just being outside in my own space has reduced my stress levels immensely and given me a completely different outlook on life which has pleasantly shocked me to be honest. I'm also surprised by the number of people I have discovered that also have allotments that I was unaware of. Colleagues at work and friends of friends etc have all come out of the closet since I joined the ranks of the Allotmenteers.

As I have developed my allotment I realise that I have developed myself. My knowledge and expertise is growing each year as I read, study and learn from trial and error and listening to the advice of my friends on the allotment has been an invaluable source of encouragement (if not always taken)

Good luck with your own personal venture and remember to enjoy every minute of it. The rewards will outweigh the disappointments in the long run – I promise!

Printed in Great Britain
by Amazon

64156176R00020